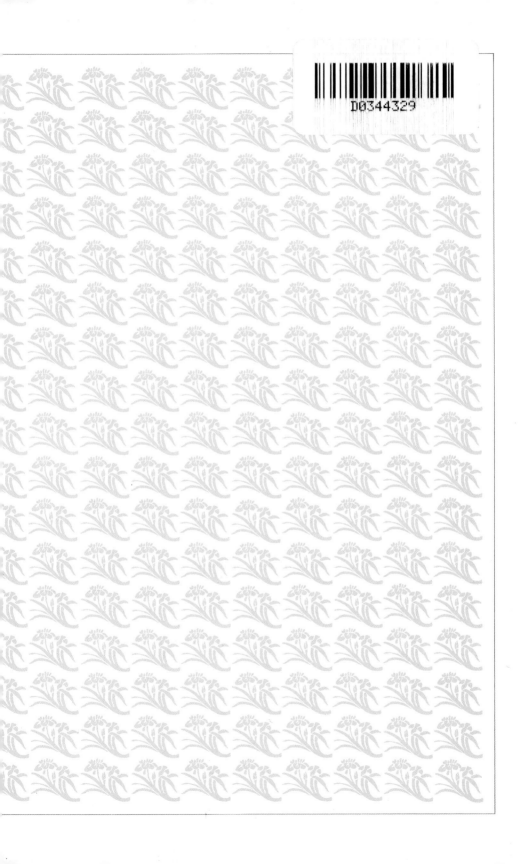

A Treasury of Friendship

A Treasury of Friendship

Hallmark Editions

Editorial Research: Harold Whaley
Editorial Direction: Aileene Neighbors

The publisher wishes to thank those who have given their kind permission to reprint material included in this book. Every effort has been made to give proper acknowledgments. Any omissions or errors are deeply regretted, and the publisher, upon notification, will be pleased to make necessary corrections in subsequent editions.

Acknowledgments: St. John 15:13; Proverbs 27:17 and 27:9-10; and Ruth 1:16-17 from the *King James Version Bible*. Reprinted by permission of the Cambridge University Press. Published by the Syndics of Cambridge University Press. "Friends!" by Thomas Curtis Clark. Reprinted by permission. "A Tribute to a Friend" by Grace Noll Crowell. Reprinted by permission of Reid Crowell. "Happy Thoughts" and "A Friend" by Mary Carolyn Davies. Reprinted by arrangement. "Winter Recompense" by Katherine Edelman. Reprinted by permission of *The Kansas City Star*. "Friend" by Elaine V. Emans. Reprinted by permission of the author. Excerpts by Hugh Black from *Words of Life*. Reprinted by permission of Harper & Row, Publishers. #1391, "They might not need me —" reprinted by permission of the publishers and the Trustees of Amherst College from Thomas H. Johnson, Editor, *The Poems of Emily Dickinson*, Cambridge, Mass.: The Belknap Press of Harvard University Press, Copyright, 1951, 1955, by The President and Fellows of Harvard College. "Thank You Note" by Gladys McKee from *Spirit*, A Magazine of Poetry, Seton Hall University, South Orange, N.J. 07079. Reprinted by permission. "Lost Friend" by Gladys McKee. First published in *McCall's* magazine. Reprinted by permission. "Invigorating Friendship" from *The Robe* by Lloyd C. Douglas. Copyright © renewed 1969 by Virginia Douglas Dawson and Betty Douglas Wilson. Reprinted by permission of the publisher, Houghton Mifflin Company. "A Friend in Need" by Henry van Dyke from *Christmas Classics* is reprinted by permission of Charles Scribner's Sons. "Miscellaneous File" by Dorothy Brown Thompson from *The Kansas City Star*. Used by permission. "Friendship" by Dorothy Brown Thompson from *Columbia*. Used by permission.

To Welcome You

Friendship — what more beautiful proof could there be that life is meant for sharing? Kindness and compassion, understanding and encouragement, trust and joy — these are the gifts that add purpose to living. And these are the gifts of a friend.

Throughout history, poets, philosophers, statesmen, writers of every calling have explored the nature and meaning of friendship. Many of their warmest and most memorable thoughts have been gathered into this exquisitely designed keepsake collection.

A Treasury of Friendship invites you to join in a celebration of one of the most delightful and inspiring relationships that can exist between human hearts. May you find this book a pleasure to read and reflect on — a lasting reminder of all that it means to have and to be a friend.

Friendship is a treasure chest
  of memories and thoughts of things
  friends have done to make life
  richer, brighter and more beautiful....
Friends are treasures more precious than
  gold or jewels.

Sister Constance Mary

For the loftiest friendships
    have no commercial element in them;
  they are founded on disinterestedness and sacrifices.
They neither expect nor desire a return for gift or service.
  Amid the tireless breaking of the billows
    on the shores of experience,
      there is no surer anchorage than a friendship
      that "beareth all things, believeth all things,
          hopeth all things."

James Fenimore Cooper

Make new friends, but keep the old;
Those are silver, these are gold.
New-made friendships, like new wine,
Age will mellow and refine.
Friendships that have stood the test —
Time and change — are surely best.
Brow may wrinkle, hair grow gray;
Friendship never knows decay.
For 'mid old friends, tried and true,
Once more we reach and youth renew.
But old friends, alas! may die;
New friends must their place supply.
Cherish friendships in your breast —
New is good, but old is best.
Make new friends, but keep the old;
Those are silver, these are gold.

Joseph Parry

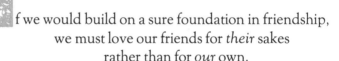

f we would build on a sure foundation in friendship,
we must love our friends for *their* sakes
rather than for *our* own.

Charlotte Brontë

6

Lost Friend

Let me lose a locket,
Money or my keys,
And I can always find a way
To substitute for these;
Let me lose a yard of time,
And I can race the sun,
Or stay up till the last pale star
And get things done;
But let me lose a friend I love,
Heart has no door nor pane,
And all the bitter winds rush in
And all the lonely rain.

Gladys McKee

Life hath no blessing like an earnest friend;
than treasured wealth more precious,
than the power of monarchs,
and the people's loud applause.

Euripides

We are advertis'd by our loving friends.

William Shakespeare

Invitation

I am content today
    here in my little room
    with lamp and fire against
    the outside cold and gloom.
I cannot keep the wide
    universe warm
    but my small room contains
    shelter from storm,
    bread of contentment,
    steeped tea to pour,
    a welcome smile and
    an unlocked door.

Marie J. Post

 mall service is true service while it lasts,
    Of humblest friends, bright creature, scorn not one;
The daisy, by the shadow that it casts,
    Protects the lingering dewdrop from the sun.

William Wordsworth

Friend is a word of royal tone;
Friend is a poem all alone.

A Persian Poet

The Perfume of Friendship

After the petals fall,
Perfume remains,
A scent in the green hall
Of country lanes.
And the clean breeze of spring
Blows over everything.

After a friend departs,
The essence of
Her spirit stirs our hearts
With faith and love.
Now she is homeward bent
Our rooms are sweet
        with friendship's sentiment.

Anne Campbell Stark

Don't flatter yourself that friendship
authorizes you to say disagreeable things to your intimates.
The nearer you come into relation with a person,
the more necessary do tact and courtesy become.

Oliver Wendell Holmes

he happiest moments of my life have been
in the flow of affection among friends.

Thomas Jefferson

The World Is Full of Beauty

The world is full of beauty —
Sparkling seas,
A garden in full bloom,
The shape of trees,
A child's eyes dancing
With some new delight,
A sky ablaze with stars
All twinkling bright,
A sun-splashed meadow's gold,
The rainbow's end...
But more than these — the love
Of friend for friend.

Katherine Nelson Davis

"Surely you cannot refuse
    what I ask in the name of our friendship!"
Then made answer John Alden:
    "The name of friendship is sacred;
What you demand in that name,
    I have not the power to deny you."
So the strong will prevailed,
    subduing and moulding the gentler,
Friendship prevailed over love,
    and Alden went on his errand.

Henry Wadsworth Longfellow

God's Best Gift

Blessed are they who have the gift of making friends,
for it is one of God's best gifts.
It involves many things,
but above all, the power of going out
of one's self, and appreciating whatever
is noble and loving in another.

Thomas Hughes

We force no doors in friendship, but like the Christ in Revelation, we stand reverently at the door without, to knock. And only if the door be opened from within, may we be welcome in to sup with our friend and he with us.

The glory of friendship is not the outstretched hand, nor the kindly smile, nor the joy of companionship; it is the spiritual inspiration that comes to one when he discovers that someone else believes in him and is willing to trust him with his friendship.

My friends have come unsought. The great God gave them to me.

Ralph Waldo Emerson

Animals are such agreeable friends —
they ask no questions.
They pass no criticisms.

George Eliot

Talisman

Friendship, in its truest sense, is next to love
the most abused of words. One may call many "friend"
and be still ignorant of that sentiment,
cooler than passion, warmer than respect,
more just and generous than either, which recognizes
a kindred spirit in another, and, claiming its right,
keeps it sacred by the wise reserve that is to friendship
what the purple bloom is to the grape,
a charm which once destroyed can never be restored.

J. Alcott

Behave toward everyone as if receiving a great guest.

Confucius

Friendship
Need never be tested;
It is just there,
Unquestioned
Like the sky, the air —
Sometimes wordless,
Even unheeded,
But there
When needed.

Betty Isler

Friends!

If all the sorrows of this weary earth —
   The pains and heartaches of humanity —
   If all were gathered up and given me,
I still would have my share of wealth and worth
   Who have you, Friend of Old, to be my cheer
   Through life's uncertain fortunes, year by year.

Thank God for friends, who dearer grow as years increase,
   Who, as possessions fail our hopes and hands,
   Become the boon supreme, than gold and lands
More precious. Let all else, if must be, cease;
   But, Lord of Life, I pray on me bestow
   The gift of friends, to share the way I go.
Thomas Curtis Clark

he ornaments of our house
     are the friends that frequent it.
Ralph Waldo Emerson

Those who bring sunshine to the lives of others
cannot keep it from themselves.
Sir James Barrie

Sonnet to John Hamilton Reynolds

O that a week could be an age, and we
Felt parting and warm meeting every week,
Then one poor year a thousand years would be,
    The flush of welcome ever on the cheek:
So could we live long life in little space,
    So time itself would be annihilate,
So a day's journey in oblivious haze
    To serve our joys would lengthen and dilate.
O to arrive each Monday morn from Ind!
    To land each Tuesday from the rich Levant!
In little time a host of joys to bind,
    And keep our souls in one eternal pant!
This morn, my friend, and yester-evening taught
Me how to harbour such a happy thought.

John Keats

When friends ask, there is no tomorrow.

Old Proverb

What is a friend?
        A single soul dwelling in two bodies.

Aristotle

friend is a present you give yourself.

Robert Louis Stevenson

A friend may well be reckoned
a masterpiece of nature.

Ralph Waldo Emerson

No Greater Blessing

There is no greater blessing
Than an understanding friend,
Who's there in times of trouble
And on whom we can depend;
A friend who knows our every mood
And brightens cloudy days;
One who's slow to criticize,
But quick to offer praise.
There is no greater blessing
Than a friend who always cares;
One who will remember us
In daily thoughts and prayers.

Kay Andrew

o man is an island, entire of itself;
    every man is a piece of the continent, a part of the main.
If a clod be washed away by the sea,
    Europe is the less, as well as if a promontory were,
      as well as if a manor of thy friends or of thine own were.
Any man's death diminishes me,
        because I am involved in mankind.
Therefore never send to know for whom the bell tolls.
    It tolls for thee.

John Donne

Friendship is the highest degree of perfection in society.

Michel de Montaigne

sleep, awake, by night or day,
    The friends I seek are seeking me;
No wind can drive my bark astray,
    Nor change the tide of destiny.

The stars come nightly to the sky,
    The tidal wave unto the sea;
Nor time, nor space, nor deep, nor high,
    Can keep my own away from me.

John Burroughs

To a Friend

I love you not only for what you are,
    but for what I am when I am with you.
I love you not only for what you have made
    of yourself, but for what you are making of me.
I love you for the part of me that you bring out.
I love you for putting your hand into my heaped-up heart
    and passing over all the foolish and frivolous
    and weak things that you can't help
    dimly seeing there, and for drawing out
    into the light all the beautiful radiant belongings
    that no one else had looked quite far enough to find.
I love you for ignoring the possibilities of the fool
    and weakling in me, and for laying firm hold
    on the possibilities of the good in me.
I love you for closing your ears to the discords
    in me, and for adding to the music in me
    by worshipful listening.
I love you because you are helping me to make
    of the timber of my life not a tavern,
    but a temple, and of the words of my every day
    not a reproach, but a song.
I love you because you have done more than any creed
    could have done to make me happy.
You have done it without a touch, without a word,
    without a sign.
You have done it first by being yourself.
After all, perhaps this is what being a friend means.

Author Unknown

What Is a Friend?

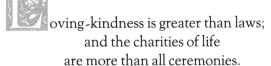friend is a person of great understanding
Who shares all our hopes and our schemes,
A companion who listens with infinite patience
To all of our plans and our dreams,
A true friend can make all our cares melt away
With the touch of a hand or a smile,
And with calm reassurance make everything brighter,
And life always seem more worthwhile —
A friend shares so many bright moments of laughter
At even the tiniest thing —
What memorable hours of lighthearted gladness
And pleasure this sharing can bring!
A friend is a cherished and precious possession
Who knows all our hopes and our fears,
And someone to treasure deep down in our hearts
With a closeness that grows through the years!

Katherine Nelson Davis

"Stay" is a charming word in a friend's vocabulary.

Amos Bronson Alcott

oving-kindness is greater than laws;
and the charities of life
are more than all ceremonies.

Talmud

Elmwood, February 27, 1867

My Dear Longfellow,

—On looking back, I find that our personal intercourse is now nearly thirty years' date. It began on your part in a note acknowledging my Class Poem much more kindly than it deserved. Since then it has ripened into friendship, and there has never been a jar between us. If there had been, it would certainly have been my fault and not yours. Friendship is called the wine of life, and there certainly is a stimulus in it that warms and inspires as we grow older. Ours should have some body to have kept so long....

I remain always affectionately yours,

James Russell Lowell

 word from a friend
     is doubly enjoyable in dark days.
Forsake not an old friend,
     for the new is not comparable unto him.

Apocrypha

Here around the ingle bleezing,
    Wha sae happy and sae free;
Tho' the northern wind blaws freezing,
    Frien'ship warms baith you and me.

Robert Burns

Ships that pass in the night,
    and speak each other in passing,
Only a signal shewn,
    and a distant voice in the darkness;
So, on the ocean of life
    we pass and speak one another,
Only a look and a voice,
    then darkness again and a silence.

Henry Wadsworth Longfellow

A mile walked with a friend
        has only one hundred steps.

Russian Proverb

Friendship is a bridge that leads
To a garden full of flowers,
Where one may spend enjoyable
And very pleasant hours —
A bridge that leads to happiness,
Companionship and pleasure,
To affection, understanding,
And to gladness without measure.

Gordon Eull

y Friend is that one whom I can associate with my choicest thought. I always assign to him a nobler employment in my absence than I ever find him engaged in, and I imagine that the hours which he devotes to me were snatched from a higher society.

Our actual Friends are but distant relations of those to whom we are pledged. We never exchange more than three words with a Friend in our lives on that level to which our thoughts and feelings almost habitually rise. O my Friend, may it come to pass once, that when you are my Friend, I may be yours.

A Friend is one who incessantly pays us the compliment of expecting from us all the virtues, and who can appreciate them in us.

The Friend asks no return but that his Friend will religiously accept and wear and not disgrace his apotheosis of him. They cherish each other's hopes. They are kind to each other's dreams.

That kindness which has so good a reputation elsewhere can least of all consist with this relation, and no such affront can be offered to a Friend, as a conscious goodwill, a friendliness which is not a necessity of the Friend's nature.

Friendship is never established as an understood relation. It is a miracle which requires constant proofs. It is an exercise of the purest imagination and of the rarest faith.

We do not wish for Friends to feed and clothe our bodies, neighbors are kind enough for that, but to do the like office to our spirit. For this, few are rich enough, however well disposed they may be.

Of what use the friendliest disposition even, if there are no hours given to Friendship, if it is forever postponed to unimportant duties and relations? Friendship is first, Friendship last.

The Friend is a *necessarius,* and meets his Friend on homely ground; not on carpets and cushions, but on the ground and rocks they will sit, obeying natural and primitive laws.

The language of Friendship is not words, but meanings. It is an intelligence above language.

Silence is the ambrosial night in the intercourse of Friends, in which their sincerity is recruited and takes deeper root.

A base Friendship is of a narrowing and exclusive tendency, but a noble one is not exclusive; its very superfluity and dispersed love is the humanity which sweetens society, and sympathizes with foreign nations; for though its foundations are private, it is, in effect, a public affair and a public advantage....

Henry David Thoreau

Thank You

ust as the outgoing tide
returns to the oceanside…
So the gift of outgoing friendship
comes back to the giver.

Cecil Nelson

And Ruth said, Intreat me not to leave thee,
or to return from following after thee:
for whither thou goest, I will go;
and where thou lodgest, I will lodge:
thy people shall be my people,
and thy God my God:
Where thou diest, will I die,
and there will I be buried:
the Lord do so to me, and more also,
if ought but death part thee and me.

Ruth 1:16-17

A Friend

A friend is one who understands,
Without ifs or maybes, buts or ands.

Mary Carolyn Davies

Then Marcellus proceeded to tell her about his finding of the Robe, and the peculiar effect it had on him. Diana looked up into his face, her eyes swimming with tears.

"There's no use trying to explain," he went on. "I gathered up the Robe in my hands — and it healed my mind."

"Maybe that was because you knew it had belonged to another lonely man," suggested Diana.

"Curiously enough," said Marcellus, "that was the sensation I had when I held the Robe in my arms. Some strange friendship — a new, invigorating friendship — had come to my rescue. The painful tension was relaxed. Life was again worth living."

Lloyd C. Douglas, THE ROBE (Chapter XXI)

Friendship is love without his wings!

Lord Byron

Friendship cannot be permanent
unless it becomes spiritual.
There must be fellowship in the deepest things of the soul,
community in the highest thoughts,
sympathy with the best endeavors.

Hugh Black

Spring Morning

Life is a spring morning
   if you've got a friend:
      someone to walk with
      and talk with
      and turn to.
Life is a spring morning
   if you've got a friend
      to share a little sun with,
      to help you along.
Now and forever…you've got a friend.

Alan Doan

The comfort of having a friend may be taken away,
but not that of having had one.

Seneca

Hello —
   a bright word
   when said with a smile,
   a happy word
   when sent with good wishes,
   a warm word
   when shared with a friend.

Mary Dawson Hughes

Friendship

Oh, the comfort — the inexpressible comfort
  of feeling safe with a person,
Having neither to weigh thoughts,
Nor measure words — but pouring them
All right out — just as they are —
Chaff and grain together —
Certain that a faithful hand will
Take and sift them —
Keep what is worth keeping —
And with the breath of kindness
Blow the rest away.

Dinah Maria Mulock Craik

Love is flower-like;
  Friendship is like a sheltering tree.

Coleridge

 ince we deserved the name of friends,
  And thine effect so lives in me,
  A part of mine may live in thee, .
  And move thee on to noble ends.

Alfred, Lord Tennyson

A Friend in Need

"A friend in need," my neighbor said to me,
"A friend indeed is what I mean to be;
In time of trouble I will come to you,
And in the hour of need you'll find me true."

I thought a bit, and took him by the hand:
"My friend," said I, "you do not understand
The inner meaning of that simple rhyme;
A friend is what the heart needs all the time."

Henry van Dyke

he only reward of virtue is virtue;
the only way to have a friend is to be one.

Ralph Waldo Emerson

I Sought My Soul

I sought my soul,
But my soul I could not see.
I sought my God,
But my God eluded me.
I sought my brother,
And I found all three.

William Blake

My Quiet Place

he world
keeps spinning, spinning,
and the days
go rushing by,
and sometimes
there is scarcely time
to stop
and wonder why.
But, inside me,
there's a quiet place
where hope and faith renew,
where the world, the world
can't reach me…
That quiet place is you.

Francee Davis

It is easy to say how we love new friends,
and what we think of them,
but words can never trace out
all the fibers that knit us to the old.

George Eliot

Some people make the world more special
just by being in it.

Mary Dawson Hughes

New Home

Across the hill this morning,
the scent of broken loam,
the steady sound of sawing
as someone builds a home.

Bright nails and hammers flashing,
a roof, a chimney place,
and then the owner watching
with eager heart and face.

A lovely field last summer,
a patch all green and still,
but now a bright new promise
of neighbors on the hill!

Marie J. Post

Greater love hath no man than this,
that a man lay down his life for his friends.

St. John 15:13

So long as we love, we serve;
so long as we are loved by others,
I would almost say that we are indispensable;
and no man is useless while he has a Friend.

Robert Louis Stevenson

It's Friendship

It's as old as man himself,
    yet as new as this moment or the next.
It's ever changing and somehow ever constant.
It's stronger than any wall ever built.
It overcomes politics and national barriers.
It can't be blinded by strange customs
    or blocked by foreign languages.
It has been written about and analyzed
    by wise men;
Yet it has never been defined, and never will be.
You can't see it or touch it, yet it is everywhere.
It survives weakness and neglect,
    thrives on thoughtfulness.
Its possibilities are infinite,
    its strength limitless.
It's what makes man human,
    what makes life worth living.
It's friendship.

Eleanor Leah Woods

Kindness in words creates confidence;
    kindness in thinking creates profoundness;
    kindness in giving creates love.

Lao-Tse

Friend

He must have heeded when a bird
Needed a broken wing renewed.
He must have walked at night, and heard
When a lost dog whined, or kittens mewed —
And comforted. He must have taken
All small things weary and forsaken
To His great heart and let them know
They had a friend indeed — for oh,
How much more does He wait for us,
Who come by our circuitous
Dim paths, to learn how glorious His
Full-flowered friendship is.

Elaine V. Emans

Let me have a friend's part
    in the warmth of your welcome
    of hand and of heart.

John Greenleaf Whittier

We cannot tell the precise moment when friendship is formed.
As in filling a vessel drop by drop,
there is at last a drop which makes it run over;
so in a series of kindnesses there is at last one
which makes the heart run over.

Samuel Johnson

Friendship

One stick will never burn alone.
  Give it its fellow,
And where it dulled as gray as stone,
  It flares in yellow.
Each time my purpose wavers low,
  A word from you can make it glow.

Dorothy Brown Thompson

I confidently expect a time when there will be seen, running like a half-hid warp through all the myriad audible and visible worldly interests of America, threads of manly friendship, fond and loving, pure and sweet, strong and lifelong, carried to degrees hitherto unknown — not only giving tone to individual character and making it unprecedentedly emotional, muscular, heroic, and refined, but having deepest relations to general politics.

Walt Whitman

 intment and perfume rejoice the heart:
so doth the sweetness of a man's friend
by hearty counsel.
Thine own friend, and thy father's friend,
forsake not....

Proverbs 27:9-10

Friends should be chosen by a higher principle of selection than any worldly one. They should be chosen for character, for goodness, for truth and trustworthiness, because they have sympathy with us in our best thoughts and holiest aspirations, because they have community of mind in the things of the soul.

Hugh Black

The finger of God
Touches your life
When you make a friend.

Lovina Naish

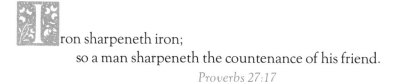

ron sharpeneth iron;
      so a man sharpeneth the countenance of his friend.

Proverbs 27:17

Everything around us — a favorite chair,
    a book, a flower — is a patient companion who,
        unlike any other friend,
           faithfully waits for the time
                when we will need it.

Paul R. Wagner

ife is a sweeter, stronger, fuller, more gracious thing for the friend's existence, whether he be near or far. If the friend is close at hand, that is best; but if he is far away he is still there to think of, to wonder about, to hear from, to write to, to share life and experience with, to serve, to honor, to admire, to love.

Arthur Christopher Benson

Like a diamond,
Friendship, with its many facets,
Is the sparkle that colors the prism of life.

Jean Grindle

But as I found you true at first,
    I find you true at last;
And now the time's a-comin'
    mighty nigh our journey's end,
I want to throw open all my soul to you,
    my friend.

James Whitcomb Riley

Thoughtfulness is a commodity that's always in demand.

Donald J. Hall

A tiny bouquet
of fresh-cut flowers
can fill a room
with sunshine....
A little act of kindness
can fill a heart
with joy.

Katherine Nelson Davis

Be courteous to all, but intimate with few,
and let those few be well tried
before you give them your confidence.
True friendship is a plant of slow growth,
and must undergo and withstand the shocks
of adversity before it is entitled to the appellation.

George Washington

True happiness consists
not in the multitude of friends,
but in their worth and choice.

Ben Jonson

God knew that everybody needs
  Companionship and cheer,
    He knew that people need someone
      Whose thoughts are always near.
He knew they needed someone kind
  To lend a helping hand,
    Someone to gladly take the time
      To care and understand…
That's why God gave us friends.

He knew that we all need someone
  To share each happy day,
    To be a source of courage
      When troubles come our way,
Someone to be true to us
  Whether near or far apart,
    Someone whose love we'll always hold
      And treasure in our hearts…
That's why God gave us friends.

Dean Walley

Said Mrs. Browning, the poet, to Charles Kingsley,
the novelist, "What is the secret of your life?
Tell me, that I may make mine beautiful also."
Thinking a moment, the beloved old author replied,
"I had a friend."

A Guest in Thought

Once a day, and sometimes more,
You knock upon my daydream door,
And I say warmly, "Come right in,
I'm glad you're here with me again!"
Then we sit down and have a chat —
Recalling this, discussing that,
Until some task that I must do
Forces me away from you —
Reluctantly I say good-bye,
Smiling with a little sigh,
For though my daydreams bring you near
I wish that you were really here —
But what reality can't change
My dreams and wishes can arrange —
And through my wishing you'll be brought
To me each day, a guest in thought.

Rowena Cox

It is a good thing to be rich,
    and a good thing to be strong,
        but it is a better thing to be loved by many friends.

Euripides

I salute you. I am your friend and my love for you goes deep. There is nothing I can give you which you have not got; but there is much, very much, that, while I cannot give it, you can take.

No heaven can come to us unless our hearts find rest in today. Take heaven! No peace lies in the future which is not hidden in this present little instance. Take peace! The gloom of the world is but a shadow. Behind it, yet within our reach, is joy. There is radiance and glory in the darkness, could we but see — and to see we have only to look. I beseech you to look.

Life is so generous a giver, but we, judging its gifts by their covering, cast them away as ugly or heavy or hard. Remove the covering and you will find beneath it a living splendor, woven of love, by wisdom, with power.

Welcome it, grasp it, and you touch the angel's hand that brings it to you. Everything we call a trial or a sorrow or a duty, believe me, that angel's hand is there; the gift is there, and the wonder of an overshadowing presence. Our joys too: be not content with them as joys. They too conceal diviner gifts.

Life is so full of meaning and purpose, so full of beauty — beneath its covering — that you will find earth but cloaks your heaven. Courage then to claim it, that is all! But courage you have, and the knowledge that we are pilgrims together, wending through unknown country, home.

Fra Giovanni

Happy Thoughts

Oh, nothing
    lovely ever ends
Upon our earth, this
    whirling star!
Enemies? They're only
    friends
Who have not yet
    found out they
    are!

Mary Carolyn Davies

The chief part of human happiness
    is derived from the society of one's fellows
    and the formation of friendships.

John Milton

A friend whom you have been gaining during your whole life,
you ought not to be displeased with in a moment.
A stone is many years becoming a ruby;
take care that you do not destroy it in an instant
against another stone.

Saadi

A Friend

A touch of the hand,
A voice on the phone,
A compliment paid,
Some sympathy shown…
A heartwarming smile,
A "Hi! How've you been?"
There's no greater joy
   than having a friend!

Mary Ellen Lowe

We can never replace a friend.
When a man is fortunate enough to have several,
he finds they are all different.
No one has a double in friendship.

Johann von Schiller

Our chief want in life is somebody
   who shall make us do what we can;
      this is the service of a friend.

Ralph Waldo Emerson

Thank You Note

It was one of those days cast in gray,
Sky and heart and the feel of the day,
And nothing minted of earth or strange
And precious fabric could make it change
Until you sent me a loaf of bread
You made yourself. I saw your head
Over a blue bowl, over a book
Reading the recipe, love in your look,
Strength in your fingers and your heart
Yielding the secret, golden part
That makes this more than fine spun wheat,
That makes the heart and the gray day sweet,
With the curious leaven one can blend
In a golden loaf of bread for a friend.

Gladys McKee

here is no better looking glass than an old friend.

Thomas Fuller

Friendship is a word,
the very sight of which in print
makes the heart warm.

Augustine Birrell

The Arrow and the Song

I shot an arrow into the air,
It fell to earth, I knew not where;
For, so swiftly it flew, the sight
Could not follow it in its flight.

I breathed a song into the air,
It fell to earth, I knew not where;
For who has sight so keen and strong,
That it can follow the flight of song?

Long, long afterward, in an oak
I found the arrow, still unbroke;
And the song, from beginning to end,
I found again in the heart of a friend.

Henry Wadsworth Longfellow

No one is rich enough to do without a neighbor.

Danish Proverb

A true friend unbosoms freely,
advises justly, assists readily, adventures boldly,
takes all patiently, defends courageously,
and continues a friend unchangeably.

William Penn

he years between
        Have taught me some sweet,
    Some bitter lessons; none
        Wiser than this — to
    Spend in all things else,
        But of old friends,
    Be most miserly.

James Russell Lowell

Life is to be fortified by many friendships. To love, and to be loved, is the greatest happiness. If I lived under the burning sun of the equator, it would be pleasure for me to think that there were many human beings on the other side of the world who regarded and respected me; I could not live if I were alone upon the earth, and cut off from the remembrance of my fellow creatures. It is not that a man has occasion often to fall back upon the kindness of his friends; perhaps he may never experience the necessity of doing so; but we are governed by our imaginations, and they stand there as a solid and impregnable bulwark against all the evils of life.

Sydney Smith

A Tribute to a Friend

You have gone the second mile so often, friend:
Beyond the line of duty you have gone!
I have found you faithful to the very end
Of every road that we have traveled on.
What can I say of gratitude and praise
Sufficient for your heart to understand:
How I have valued you throughout the days,
Your cheering words, your ever-steadying hand?

"God bless you, friend." Perhaps this ancient prayer
May work some shining miracle for you.
God grant it may be so as He moves there
To work for you. I pray that He may do
Some wonder thing, some blessing that will be
A bright reward for all you mean to me.

Grace Noll Crowell

A friend is somebody you want to be around
when you feel like being by yourself.

Barbara Burrow

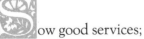ow good services;
sweet remembrances will grow from them.

Madame de Staël

Fruit of Friendship

The whole fruit of friendship is in the love itself,
for it is not the advantage, procured through a friend,
but his love itself that gives delight.

Marcus Tullius Cicero

The desire for friendship is strong in every human heart. We crave the companionship of those who can understand. The nostalgia of life presses, we sigh for "home," and long for the presence of one who sympathizes with our aspirations, comprehends our hopes and is able to partake of our joys. A thought is not our own until we impart it to another, and the confessional seems a crying need of every human soul. The desire for sympathy dwells in every human heart.

We reach the divine through someone, and by dividing our joy with this one, we double it, and come in touch with the universal. The sky is never so blue, the birds never sing so blithely, our acquaintances are never so gracious as when we are filled with love for someone.

Elbert Hubbard

Once let friendship be given that is born of God, nor time nor circumstance can change it to a lessening; sometimes we are blessed with one who sees through us, as Michael Angelo saw through a block of marble, when he attacked it in a divine fervor, declaring that an angel was imprisoned within it; — and it is often the delicate, resolute hand of such a friend that sets the angel free. There are soul-artists who go through this world looking among their fellows with reverence, as one looks among the dust and rubbish of old shops for hidden works of Titian and Leonardo da Vinci, and finding them, however cracked and torn and painted over with tawdry daubs of pretenders, immediately recognize the divine original, and set themselves to cleanse and restore.

Harriet Beecher Stowe

desire to conduct the affairs of this administration
so that if at the end,
when I come to lay down the reins of power,
I have lost every other friend on earth,
I shall have at least one friend left,
and that friend shall be down inside of me.

Abraham Lincoln

Winter Recompense

inter whines
At our windowpane,
Snow shrouds pines
And hides each lane,
But there's time for sewing,
A book, a game —
Time for friendship glowing
Near a bright hearth flame.

Katherine Edelman

It is great to have friends when one is young,
  but it is still more so when you are getting old.
When we are young, friends are, like everything else,
  a matter of course.
In the old days we know what it means to have them.

Edvard Grieg

A friend is the first person who comes in
when the whole world has gone out.

Author Unknown

When true friends meet in adverse hour,
'Tis like a sunbeam through a shower.
A watery way an instant seen,
The darkly closing clouds between.

Sir Walter Scott

What a wonderful way
for a day
to begin…
When a door swings wide
and a friend says:
"Come in!"

Cecil Nelson

They might not need me — yet they might;
I'll let my heart be just in sight
A smile so small as mine, might be
Precisely their necessity.

Emily Dickinson

If only all the hands that reach could touch….

Mary A. Loberg

56

Just why should friends be chronological,
Fraternal friends, or pedagogical,
Alike in race or taste or color —
It only makes the meetings duller!
Unclassified by tribe or steeple,
Why shouldn't friends be merely people?

Dorothy Brown Thompson

A smile is a light in the window
 of a face that signifies
The heart is at home and waiting.
Nothing on earth can smile but man.
Gems may flash reflective light,
 but what is the flash of a diamond
Compared with a flash of a smile?
A face that cannot smile
 is like a bud that cannot blossom.
It withers and dies on its stalk.
Laughter is day. Sobriety is night.
And the smile is the twilight
That hovers gently between both,
More bewitching than either.

Henry Ward Beecher

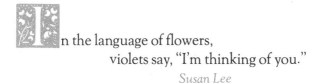n the language of flowers,
violets say, "I'm thinking of you."

Susan Lee

There are few subjects which have been more written upon, and less understood, than that of friendship. To follow the dictates of some, this virtue, instead of being the assuager of pain, becomes the source of every inconvenience. Such speculatists, by expecting too much from friendship, dissolve the connection, and by drawing the bands too closely, at length break them.

Oliver Goldsmith

Old friends, old scenes, will lovelier be
As more of Heaven in each we see.

John Keble

A friend is a gift
whose worth cannot be measured
except by the heart.

Mary Harmon

Special Thoughts From Special Friends

Set in Goudy Old Style Italic,
a typeface designed by Frederic W. Goudy
and introduced in 1916.
The paper is Hallmark Eggshell.
Designed by Lavonia Harrison and Myron McVay.

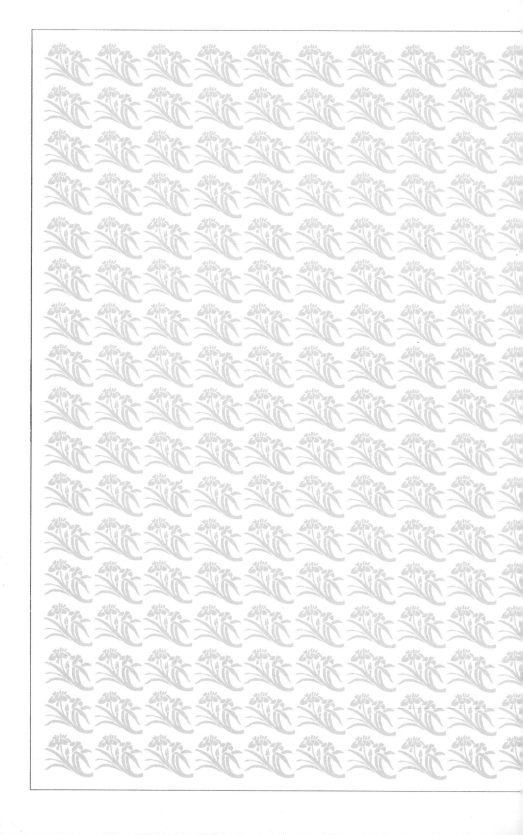